D0912956

Slow Music

OTHER BOOKS BY

GENEVIEVE TAGGARD

Poetry

    For Eager Lovers
    Hawaiian Hilltop
    Words for the Chisel
    Traveling Standing Still
    Not Mine to Finish
    Calling Western Union
    Collected Poems, 1918–1938
    Long View

Biography

    The Life and Mind of Emily Dickinson

Anthologies edited

    May Days
    Continent's End (*with James Rorty and George Sterling*)
    Circumference, Varieties of Metaphysical Verse
    Ten Introductions (*with Dudley Fitts*)

Pamphlets

    Falcon
    A Part of Vermont

Slow Music

By

Genevieve Taggard

Harper & Brothers Publishers

NEW YORK AND LONDON

1946

WG1 E

58877
811.5-T125s

COPYRIGHT, 1943, 1944, 1945, 1946, BY GENEVIEVE TAGGARD. PRINTED
IN THE UNITED STATES OF AMERICA. ALL RIGHTS IN THIS BOOK ARE
RESERVED. NO PART OF THE BOOK MAY BE REPRODUCED IN ANY MANNER
WHATSOEVER WITHOUT WRITTEN PERMISSION EXCEPT IN THE CASE OF
BRIEF QUOTATIONS EMBODIED IN CRITICAL ARTICLES AND REVIEWS.
FOR INFORMATION ADDRESS HARPER & BROTHERS

9 – 6

FIRST EDITION

H – V

Contents

I

Song I   3
The Weed   4
Demeter   5
Delight   6

II

This Poem   9
Hymn to Yellow   10
The Experience of Memory   11
Song II   12
Remote Design   13
Report on a War   14
Poet   15
Vision of River and Gulf   17

III

Evangel   21
Song III   22
Charm for a Young Private   23
Lullaby   24
To My Sister, Ernestine Kealoha Taggard, 1900–1943   25
Gilfeather Again   26
True Fable   27
The Smile   28
The Geraniums   29
The Family   30

[v]

IV

Song IV   33
Angel in Mascara   34
The Little Girl with Bands on Her Teeth   35
In the Tail of the Scorpion   36
Dialogue on Cider   37
A Poem to Explain Everything about a Certain Day in
    Vermont   39
A Sombrero is a Kind of Hat—This Poem is a Kind of Non-
    sense   40
Problem of Evil into Cocoon   42

V

Andalucía   45
Cante Hondo   47
Salute to the Russian Dead   49
With Beat of Drum   51
Song V   52
From Sybil Nation's Notebook   53
Aleatory Wind   54

VI

Exchange of Awe   59
The Zig Zag Song   62

I am indebted to Dudley Fitts for his helpful criticism of the manuscript of this book.

G. T.

*"Numberless are the world's wonders, but none
More wonderful than man. . . ."*

        —SOPHOCLES

"Praised be the fathomless universe. . . ."

        —WHITMAN

Acknowledgment

These poems were first published in: *Accent, Arizona Quarterly, Christian Register, Kenyon Review, New Yorker, New Masses, Poetry, A Magazine of Verse, Saturday Review of Literature, Sewanee Review, Virginia Quarterly,* and *Quarterly Review of Literature.*

Some of these poems have been previously published in *A Part of Vermont,* The River Press, East Jamaica, Vermont.

Salute to the Russian Dead was written for the Congress of American Soviet Friendship and read by Margaret Webster at the Congress November 8, 1942.

G. T.

I

Song I

I was a bell and I was still.
Hooded with dark, cold clapper-tongue.
I was a bell and I was still.

The air was hooded, the air was stone.
The air grew sombre when no bell was rung,
The air was hooded, the air was stone.

I was the air, I was the stone.
I broke the air and the stone; and the bell
Began to hum with the hum of bronze.

The air was nimble and all agroan,
And rang with the agony of the bell.
And joy was born in echo-bronze.

I am that joy, tip-dulcet of tone,
The thrill of the bell I am; and the still
Lip of the bell.
                    Calm, calm I clang.

1943

The Weed

My sister loved milkweed, flower and plant,
Bland-toned, upsprung. The odd dim smell,
Faint fuchsia drench of color coated white
In the brown weed clusters.
                    Sister, I can't
Find you on all the long hard walks of the night . . .
(Travail of lost person always hunted for.)
Day shows the visible universe, humbles to this:
Comfort, great weed.
                    I circle down . . .
Cluster, odor, color: blast of green wind from the earth's
          great core.

1943

Demeter

In your dream you met Demeter
Splendid and severe, who said: Endure.
Study the art of seeds,
The nativity of caves.
Dance your gay body to the poise of waves;
Die out of the world to bring forth the obscure
Into blisses, into needs.
In all resources
Belong to love. Bless,
Join, fashion the deep forces,
Asserting your nature, priceless and feminine.
Peace, daughter. Find your true kin.
              —then you felt her kiss.

1945

Delight

IN THE secret place of the heart
What is it my heart most cherishes?
What image, what toto in dream, what token held in tight
    fingers?
O, one from sweet everyday, whereon I dart
Like a child, whereon no joy perishes,
Wherein no fatal bitterness lingers.

My tall man walking the meadow at night, with the lantern,
A solemn sleepy procession, he and I to the cabin,
Both silent, I at his heels, to return
In morning dew, in first sunrays, with the dark lantern.

And if I were Ariel come home from toils and circling
    errands,
I could laugh no more sweetly than when I inwardly see it,
My delight a trembling frame to this Attic picture.

Stern world, one rollicking image, for around this happy
    thing
Forever I turn in light handsprings of the spirit.

1943

2

This Poem

THIS poem,—(which contains
A world which contains a poem,
This poem which contains a poem and a versal world,
Bubble in bubble)—this poem
Must be read in a moment and
Felt in less than a moment for
Its self is evanescent. Not so, the earth.
How solid it is. And see
Issuing from the atomy globe
A phantom, kneeling and rising, forever enchanting.
It is the crisis-cross fume of our notion of her.
Who knows: is she an immortal bomb burning its fuse-
    instant?
Never to burst? Who knows? She burns at the touch of our
    minds.
We, the art of her jargon, her marvel of marvels,
Her mastering zeal, aspire . . . In this we suffer much
And live only when we are one, "unfolded out of the folds."
Hail, hail, unholy mother; and hail, our glory.
This is Tuesday morning; and we, the multitude
Fresco the wall of the sky into which we fade.

1944

Hymn to Yellow

LA, LA, LA. To live with, to be like, to be
The serene, the level color. At ease in being. Of illusion clean.
Here is our kind. Parable of the bee's departure
On a swoon of air, lifted, guided, beguiled
To a bonfire of bloom, the yellow crest, la, la, la.
Corona horizon, utter pure, utter glow texture,
Flower goal nodding; new era's flange, la, la.

Translate us here, with the bee's literal urge,
Our lives soft bullets to this target, peace.
Large ritual—satisfaction luminous to no fraud.
Human burial, unalone, in quiet color accrued.
La, la, la into sepulcher, la, la into yellow,
Exuberance passing on, la, la, la,
Bold and bland into deathless change, the cool petal.

Bury us not in foaming snow, bury us not in brown,
Scatter us not in ash, sluice us not in green veins.
We decline to inhabit ideal blue. Divest us of love's blood,
Of red, and the splashes of rage.
                    But bury us like the bee
In calyx of yellow: to eat, to venerate the pollen, to eat
Particles, motes, specks of the dust, the yellow secret
Vibration:—living and dying in the sun's clear delicate ray.

1943

The Experience of Memory

HABITUAL sadness has its insect note,
Quake-ecstasy, its open quiet, timed.
I recall
Too clearly, discord and quarrel,
Lost friends with malice in their eyes
When I hear the jay's tiresome voice, or observe
Blue motions threading the young pines, several and blue,—
Moving over acres of memory, into the edges of legend,
The glister of pain—birds all color-crest.
Is it the flash of the still-loved person,
Or the inebriate cry of the jay?
Yah, sharply here they come,
Ventriloquist birds, on arrowy wings upheld
To harpy the self,—with flicks of mirror blue.

1944

Song II

O BEAUTIFUL and possible and necessary,
Necessary and possible,
Soon to be beautiful.
In the vigor of arms, lapse of sorrow's voice.
Now to arrest the iridescent rage of the child,
Now to accost the amazement, the apathy, the lag
In the broken adult:
The varnish-brown of timid death.
Accosting all events, contrary, grotesque,
Evading hysteria, fearing no evil . . .
O beautiful and possible and necessary,
Necessary and possible,
Soon to be beautiful.

1945

Remote Design

NOTHING lives in the circle
but the red cape, red, red, red,
the cape with fluted edges
turning on the axis of a still body,
a dream torso.
In the trance
of the circuit arena, round, round, round,
the cape lances clean
an ambit of air. Then ah! ah! diagonal and tangent
interrupts, el toro.

1943

Report on a War

WE, under giant hand, blank size of the fubbed dark,
Under giant foot, an also-hand,
A scuff, a lagging claw,
A backward member, searching criss and cross,
Plucking at shards for fun
In the huge glove of dark . . .
This enormous nothing made us not.
And we lay flat.
Brain on horizon, sensing the sky fallen,
Flat on horizon, throbbing, the guns sullen,
Membrane blows, distant and at random . . .
And pocking ruin like a scud of hail.

1945

Poet

TRAGIC meaning was my altitude.
Took it for mine, felt it lift
Very high, learned to live holding it behind diamond eyes,
In brain, in balance, let it eat at the vitals,
Seeing and willing events in crystal focus:
Large stars convening for nativity-eve.

Then saw the magnetic hope, and saw
Rays of power. From the saffron corpse of the tragic
Saw the new babe born, lusty, contorted.
Saw cohorts of cloud circling, dispersing,
Again circling; and space circling the perilous birth,
Until peril deepened, stained hope's country scarlet.

So refused the usual small role, knowing the nature,
The large terrain of the time. Since it is vision, since it is
Mine to say what it is, how quiet the eyes
Seeing, and the mouth open and saying:
This time, these people, the crisis hurrying
Near the defile of the evil story, this, soon and new.

Then dare to descend as by parachute, sheer
Drop down to place assigned, sheer down to fact.
Completely to relinquish vision and its piercing virtue.
Fall to the weight of one day with one life for gift.
Drawing the line from zenith to earth's tiny inches.
Suffer the limitation of beginning action. So on

Linked in unit of slow going; in the line as it stops;
With stop after step, the signal awaited. One
In the lock with all, chained but never slave.
Here sweat out struggle nothing-sweeter than history.
Web of feet working over dark bloody ground.
Heart plunging neatly, spasm on spasm.

1943

Vision of River and Gulf

SLIM shapes of ether, birds drawn in to vortex
Down the Mississippi, with thin on-going wing
First sped. Entire autumn's count.
A canopy of speed, uncoiling flag
Over the muddy verge. Then began
That other vision, the burial of song.
All the mute poets of the continent
Asleep, their revolutionary selves afloat,
All, since the beginning came, and each by each
Stretched in its corpse went down the turgid flood.
Over them coursed the birds, under them water, water.
Then came the dispossessed to crowd the bank.
A spell, a trance, as of an arid day
Fell on their woeful looks; and one by one
The poets in their rigor swept them by.
And they, at last, upon the bank, they sang.
The river cleared to crystal and the gulf
Swept corpses by and all the birds dispersed.
Up stood the hosts, the human everlasting
Hosts, rising at the continent's heart,
The human future in tall bodies born.
Then with that downward force, the sad swept down,
Drowned multitude on multitude, to churn
The gulf electric blue, of grief devoid,
To breed the storm, mixed from the crystal purge,
And from their dark community, swept down,
The darting cyclone came.

1944

3

Evangel

"He's the lily of the valley,
The bright and morning star. . . ."
In the world of the poor
Lily means lily,
Valley means valley.
Bright and morning star
Means Jesus.
Jesus means rescue.
This song the poor share.
The poor know no art
But that lily is lily,
Misery misery,
That Jesus is love,
That love is as rare as lilies,
And fair as the morning star.

1944

Song III

SING for the lonely. Or write the lonely a letter.
Touch the typewriter gently when you tap out the first line,
 the second.

If you sing, give the guitar a caress, a little slap of the fingers.
Sing for the lonely.

So much is false in the world; so much is shoddy.
The lonely are many; who has not met them
On the streets of the world, in a stream of everyday faces,
Burdened, gentle, cherished by no one. . . .

Sing now for the lonely, or write the lonely a letter.
Touch the typewriter gently when you tap out the first line,
 the second.
If you sing, give the guitar a caress, a little slap of the
 fingers.
Sing for the lonely.

1943

Charm for a Young Private

SAY goodbye to all you love,
Kiss all you love goodbye;
And take with you as you go
All you love, compressed, to keep,
Whether you live or die.
The rule of war will throw
All you love in the play with chance,
Where Death will fly in the air.
Come back from the nightmare sleep,
Survive, if you may, the nightmare
And find all you love in a trance,
                And the new world fair.

1942

Lullaby

(for music)

HUSH, new child, how
Give you good love?
(You now so new.)
How be gentle now
Unless, in love, the stress
Inward from wide tenderness
Turns, like a pure wave, wide
Gliding from under the world, from its farthest side
In softening rings.
Loving all; foreign, small,
Sad and never seen.

                         (Hush, children, while Mother sings.)

And so
Floats the new one on an endless flow
Breathing pure air.
How give you good love, new and so rare,
(hush), but so?

1943

To My Sister—Ernestine Kealoha Taggard,
1900-1943

WE now alive, live as we can
And feel the final wound, and all deny:
. . . Your lessening speech, the periods of space
Outspread. Waiting the tranced reply.
And now in no direction turn
To hear the answer with the little sigh.
This waste of space all wandering with no cry.

O lovely sphinx, imperative of moods,
As when you stood in doorway when we turned,
Or on the path in the late littered woods,
And smiled and walked apart, who still refuse
As if you heard but had not heart to choose
The word to speak. So Silence has
Made all yourself his answer of one phrase.

1943

Gilfeather Again

In Gilfeather pasture, trim with moss
Near leafy mingle, in cove of air,
Space, by our moving, flows across
Meadow to shadow, and softly, there
Evening birds exchange by rote
Perfected oddments, echo-pure.
I hear them open on one note
Serene, secure.

No hurt retreats us from this calm,
Now fragile, and so seasonal.
Here, healing as the scriptural balm
In Gilead, affirms the small
Invisible thrush with delicate throat—
Where we delay or return to hear it—
Of which the importunate psalmist wrote
For the broken spirit.

1943-1945

True Fable

Now make one fable of the source of love:
What finger of fire, they ask, what idiot luck,
In a waste of cults and bones and empty men. . . .
It was poetry, poetry and the human heart.

And when a child, what filled you most with awe?
Found you a magnet-center, a golden test?
The burning bush, and the pathos of a voice:
It was poetry, poetry and the human heart.

Child loves the dazzle-frond, jumps up and down,
Not knowing flame, certain of its want,
Quick in the person of the syllables:
Poetry, poetry and the human heart.

O, long ago the keen delighting lit
An answering fire, the only deathless love,
Breathing and quiet—an inward delicate sense:
Poetry, poetry, and the human heart.

1940

The Smile

LET us not wrongly honor archaic good
That quickens to evil in the crux of change,
Except to revere its past, except to see
Virtue reborn and renamed, in the color of blood.

Goodness, your wrinkled face is dear and strange.
How deeply in myself you transfigure me,
Permitting me kinship in a brotherhood
To which man's durable virtue is the key.

Call them not wise who curse our times and brood
In horror of man, and horror of solitude.
Revere we must, who are native to this good,
Profound to discover your face smiling through change.

1945

The Geraniums

EVEN if the geraniums are artificial
Just the same,
In the rear of the Italian café
Under the nimbus of electric light
They are red; no less red
For how they were made. Above
The mirror and the napkins
In the little white pots . . .
. . . In the semi-clean café
Where they have good
Lasagne. . . . The red is a wonderful joy
Really, and so are the people
Who like and ignore it. In this place
They also have good bread.

1946

The Family

THE sadness of the old, the veteran old
Purges the crude
Metal. Purges the headlong blood
Of its one-word reply. The old
Say nothing wild.
But take up children in the lap to sit,—
Spent out of person in this clean defeat,
To blunder love and argue action true,
Until the planets hoist them, until they lift
Big on horizons in the chairs of sky,
Rocking, forever rocking in their parlor blue,
—Sober ring of rocking, critical few . . .

So shine the ancients in the wintering void.

1946

4

Song IV

ILL is her life, level and mean,
Yet her ways are all serene.
Her spirit is primrose,
And all repose.
Too satin-sunny for a noisy joy,
Too lambent for cold-color shows,
Halcyon yellow amid the yelling of hoodlums.

So she could sit in hell,
Her skull and bones egg-shell,
Her small arms hanging down.
Such a limpid hopeless gold
In the corrupt cold
Of hell, the desolate evil still in the same ratio:
Halcyon yellow amid the yelling of hoodlums.

1945

Angel in Mascara

WHEN first she came to see me
My thoughts were crazy as death.
When next she came to see me,
"I like not Nazareth,"
I said, "I live with the poor in spirit.
Our life is death."

Behold the pretended angel
Recoiling at my word.
Behold the golden evangel
Poised, with avenging sword.
"Witch," I cried, "Marauder,
I go beyond the word."

"Where go you then, where go you?"
"I go for the bliss of wealth."
"O evil one and selfish,"
She cried with icy stealth,
Crazy in her unhealth.
Her strong arts ripped like water,
And hordes unhid her wealth.

1945

The Little Girl With Bands on Her Teeth

I WAS far forward on the plain, the burning swamp,
When the child called. And she was far behind.
She was not my child, my charge. By chance I heard.
She called from the first delusive fork. She cried her distress.
For me, much walking lay ahead, my stint, much walking.
The very gist of the problem. And nightfall. And I in a
    swamp.
I heard, could not go on; she cried; she called me back.

Then my temper was short, for remember I split my duty in
    two.
Any cry is the concern of all; we are all in a swamp . . . this
    was discovered.
But the old fables of ruin decline. . . . I deserted myself.
Once to go back is nothing; one return matters not,
But daily to traverse the great gap of our ages,
Daily to go on, and daily return the triple mile!
And she less able to go . . . to see her less able.

Good Christopher, the saint! Bless the past for such pity.
The windows of pity shine, holy and vapid.
We need an essential plinth in the gap of that pity.
Farewell, Child. Try to hear my bleak meaning.
We will build a fine house, if we finish this journey.
My specious pride dies. If you wish, call me evil.
I travel the risk of the end. O perilous love.

1944

In the Tail of the Scorpion

A SUAVE and paltry man, my enemy,
He encounters no spirit law to lay him low.
Thrives in his pose, lustrous where I wilt,
Pretender in a trivial charade.

Robs me and daunts me, to a meanness down.
Still there's no base to put my rage upon.
"No being is half so paltry. Search for depth."
O zero-hero of my hate and love!

Who in this splendid universe of smart
Summer equipment can make moral sense
Where men are folded down like garden chairs,
And whiffs of autumn fleck canary paint.

1946

Dialogue on Cider

FORGIVE me, but I want to go
To Canada and Mexico.

Be still, be still. What would you see?

People.

           But wherefore go
To Canada and Mexico?

People are mysteries to me.

There are they less mysterious?

Here, I dare not; but there I guess . . .

You'll never *Know*.

But I desire to peek and peer
At people not disguised by *here*.
Perhaps I know too much to see
All that I should. I want them clear.

You want them quaint. That won't do.
Stay home until your eyes are sure.
Travel is never any cure.

My itching foot still wants to go
To Canada and Mexico.

That's an excuse. I think you want
To get away from old Vermont.

You have a touch of vertigo.
What would you see?

Places.

Why do that?

This planet is my habitat.
I like the shiver in Labrador.
I like the air of North.
The mango calls for me to go
To pink and yellow Mexico.

Such things to travel for!
Well go for all of me.

I'm setting forth.
Popocatepetl smokes
And Canada is full of oaks.

And the world of fools.
After that what will you do?

After I have gone, la, la,
To Mexico and Canada,
Gone and come again, I want
To lay me down in old Vermont.

To die?

To die.
But first to go
To Canada and Mexico.

Why?
Goodbye!

1945

A Poem to Explain Everything About
a Certain Day in Vermont

FIFTY wizards working in the wind
And one tall wizard standing in their rear
Made a quick sheen to lacquer all Vermont.
Up leapt the sun. The air was far and near.

The weeds, the grass, the corn, the slipping river
Made wizard-quiet. My noon-sleepy deer
Whisked in the shade, saw winsome sun go over,
And still those wizards brewed the atmosphere.

The lone tall wizard opened up the west.
Sunset made its exit beryl and sheer.
Those wizards leapt like acrobats, swinging free,
Hung their thin capes upon cold Vega's spear. . .

Galaxies were thick, weather was clear.

1944

A Sombrero   Is a Kind of Hat   This Poem
Is a Kind of Nonsense

THE sombre man in sombrero
Made no sign to stay or go
When he called. He sat
He and his hat,
The sombre man.

Is he a political Jo
Who came to call in sombrero?
(But not with his hat in hand.
Oh no.
Shirt and hat he kept on.)
He wants to know where we stand.

(Is he Bill Buffalo? . . .
Is he bad and good
Like Robin Hood
And Jesse James? . . .)

Speaking of wonderful names
Perhaps he is Prospero
Or someone like that. Now he haunts
Little boys, in little boy stunts.
Off with your dreams, little boys.
And cut off the radio.
The sombre man says so.
He is sombre and tired of noise.

Outlaw and cowboy are gone
Who wore the rebel sombrero

Who pranced under circles of shadow.
Here is a thoughful man,
An exceeding discreet fellow.
We end where we began
With the sombre man.

1945

Problem of Evil into Cocoon

ARE monsters all big?
I connive on a twig,
Head to heel, head to heel,
Aloof in chenille.
Arrogant worm, is my name,
Ugly worm, they exclaim.
I warp to a hood.
I filter no good.
As horror as whale,
Malignant as eel,
As stinging, as male
In a sheath of chenille.

So fester on dews,
On my moss of chartreuse.
And if men come me nigh
Make a fright for near eye.
Arrogant worm, is my name.
Ugly worm, they exclaim.
Next make, next transform
Me more evil than worm.
My stupor I obey:
Erupt will I from this sack,
Monster as huge as day
And black as night is black.

1943

5

Andalucía

SILENCE like light intense,
Silence the deaf ear of noise . . .
The hid guerrillas wishing to commence
The big war, the war of the full voice.
In rocks, knives, guns, and dynamite,
. . . Or the scratch of scorpions ticking in the night;
And at the church door near the altar boys
One in black frowns with a boy in white . . .

Andalucía, land of naked faces.
Country of silver and green sky; lonely country, country of
    throngs.
Arabia and Africa in gardens and in arid places.
Country of essential dances and the song of songs.
Andalucía, place of the wine yellow light;
Place of wind too lucid for hissing in small tones.
Andalucía, where our dead comrades are young bones,
The color of old rock mountains, bone yellow and white.

In Andalucía it is
Now a country of silences
Since the war; a hiss
Is the way of the wind,
And what a man says
Is also in his silences,
In the glance he gives behind
In Andalucía, land of naked silences.

Andalucía, you too will feel
The wide wind that unlocks systems:

[45]

Franco to skid his heels and reel,
Men to shudder on the cluttered Thames.
A great rushing across the planet drives
Breath into bodies. Shouts and arms awake.
Andalucía, country of silver and green, shake
Like a reclaimed cloak, hum like a city of hives.

In Andalucía it is
Now a country of silences
Since the war; a hiss
Is the way of the wind,
And what a man says
Is also in his silences,
In the glance he gives behind,
In Andalucía, land of naked silences.

1943

Cante Hondo

IT IS the demon wail.
The deepest pit of man casts out this voice,
Wail, repeated, partaking . . .
Red blood crying its art from the ground.
On prison wall
Streak and stain of song
Trickling today's blood. Innermost red, the old
Crying from burial,—Arab and Phoenician,
Re-echoed crying
From the never never people
Crying.

Parts doubled oddly, to evade death
Or the tyrant hand.
Woman with the voice of man,
Man with the voice of woman,
Spear and rose, rose and spear,
So woman and man transpose
In the organs of breath.

Feet held back from dancing,
Action withheld into rest
O world-shaking moment of inaction
In fire and breath.

Will the race end in the noose of its suffering, end
Clutched in unspilled blood, in its black care?

Throat open; red guitar
Bowing before the throat,

Bowing before the ear
Hurtling spear-note throbbing. Gigantic throat
In naked diamond formal sobbing.
Olé, Olé, Olé
Falsetto suffering. *O*
Adelante, Adelante

Olé.

Throat open; red guitar
Bowing before the throat,
Its spear-note throbbing . . .
She, she is that demon-male, that bronze restraint,
She of the throat.

Adelante.

The demon sobbing.
And in alternate throat
Male,—lament on long lament, in shattered wail,—
Human-woman quiver. He
Of the throat
Falsetto-male. O sexual song.

1945

Salute To the Russian Dead

GENIUS is like radium. A drop held in hand
Burns . . . Stuff of incandescence, of rarity, diamond, alive . . .
This, diffused in the blood of men in the ranks,
In the step of millions, in the hands
That serve the huge machinery of war . . .

Genius, running red on the wads of grass, sodding the crisp
     weeds,
Stain-darkening spring flowers, painting and spattering the
     snow-terrain,
Genius in the blood, pumped from the human heart
Through delicate thin veins . . .
                And so is genius delicate,
Quick to die like grass and quick to weary like the body,
Needing cheer and sustenance like a child at the breast . . .

Now in this war genius is as common as red, genius quickens
In all and takes the color of blood. It is passion.
It will give itself utterly. It will not turn slave.
It is red and human and hot.
             This planet
Is nothing without this hero-beating heart.

A few writers die near the front and we are sorry.
Artists suffer—but not as artists. All suffer.
We remember that all men must die. We remember
That these did not die sorry for their deaths.

For those who never made books or small poems,
We will cry loudly, feeling an agony in this necessity.
Whatever is good and tangible and fair in time to come
Begins here, where they die in their blood, in their genius.

1942

With Beat of Drum

LET the poem be like a drum,
Let it have heart-beat,
Let it have heart.
The age into which we come
Demands the large
Movement, wants marching feet.
Let the poem be a part
Of the age, a part of each
Marching citizen,—
To link in sound, to keep his fluid run
Part of the large, the age, one-many in the one.
Help him, in need, in the last charge.
Give him comfort, find him unity.
Give him the strength of ten,
The simplicity of Hallelujah and Amen.
Thudding drum, rally and rouse
Him, rally and rouse
Him to himself. Accent the scope of one.
Then end, for you are done.
Now, in your quiet, the maturity of the nation.
Now all men welcome in the ample house,—
All, under the ample, the expanding sun . . .
Rose-fruits of peace, the flags, the sunset gun:
Landscape of the citizen.

1943

Song V

In unjust, cyclonic series
In event upon event
This war-world crested them
Over the edge, to death.

And with death-dealing furies
The casual-hearted went.
Our indecision wrested them
To numb degrees of faith.

Charnel sea, invade us,
Cyclone, cleanse us.
Justice, levy us.
Marshal, employ us.

1944

From Sybil Nation's Notebook

In the Continuum
The Norm
Comprehends
The Extremes. Leave the extremes, try
For your maturity,
Resumption, duration,
Unbroken sequence: study
The ant, the spider, the Mississippi.
Avoid, avoid
That splitting wraith who now conducts
To short mad flights, abrupt self-made defeats.
Only essence, essence of continuum
And nothing short of this is sense, in essence.
Staunch is the word. The verb
Will serve for wounds;
Love and work attain
Its very nature.

1944

Aleatory Wind

Much offends,
Especially the new beauty;
The honest eye that shines and pierces
Even while it pours its honest love like a vapor of healing.
The bare ritual offends;
And the ritual of brotherhood
Which is the basalt sense of the world
Offends, is made to seem contrary and ugly
By means of another ritual with a flimsy deity
And a fantastic logic.
                    Where the hands have no liking
For stones and where minds are blind
To structure. Wherever the hands cease to take hold,
Where the mind backs away from the plain and the related.
This ritual will hurt
The hands of those
Who have left the wilderness of necessity,
Deep mutuality, the sense of distance,
The sense of depth.

Of the fertility of stones, their tears.
Of the electrical star, its tears.
Of the hilarity of the stone brotherhood, the activity
     of jasper,
Of the inertia of stones, the fixity of basalt,
Of the vigor of stones in their power to draw,
To test metals, to build shapes, to be in space,
To become fluid in the blood of volcanoes,
Of these I made claim . . .

"No art," said the European, sidestepping the rattlesnakes,
With ballet steps. "Unreal," said the European, "No ghosts.
No culture."

I took a stone of weeping in my right hand.
And a stone of laughter in my left.
So the ritual always began, testing the power to hold.
Holding them behind me I juggled them evenly and said
    "Choose.
Lodestones and touchstones. Magnets subtle, complex.
The greathearted jewels of the obsidian world."

And looking downward I saw a finger of wind in the dust,
Spinning the dust in a wheel, erratic,
In a funnel, a nothing of wind.

New-world dust sang a sulky little song,
But the tourist heard no song
And saw only liver-colored dust
About a foot high, suspended, in which to wade.

This stone is the electrical star,
The cleaver of space; can you, will you
Bowl it in nine-pins?
Curve it, will it to glide
In dream repetition?

We learn slowly the ritual of stones
And the tactile sense. The snap of action.
The excellent flash of the body
When it kneels and swings.

In this ritual we dance.
For we clasp our ghost, we whirl with a new music.
He is the man we murdered,
The red man. He goes. He is here.
Our ghost is our culture. And we embrace another.
He is the man we murder.
The black man. He returns and returns,
Teaching ritual. And every kind of man
Draws into this whirl. The wind veers
As if to nullify all.
The center of the earth is basalt.

Here we gaze to commune
On action's articulate bones,
Observing our guilt; the rituals of food and power
All wrongly played. Of this we know much.
Sharing aleatory wind
A thin ether,
Playing with skulls, color, gadgets
Inventions and dice.

A dangerous country. With a culture like whisky.

The European wore gloves,
And under the gloves, thimbles
On each finger—clumsy.
He turned the pages of old situations
And muttered his pity in the stony places.

1945

6

Exchange of Awe

DEEP cup of this cave
Heeds the moon,
Heeds the sun, tips down and up
With the tides. (So the cave rides,
The world, all gilded, glides.)
With sun, tide, moon,
With orb, quarter, crescent and the crescent wave,
Asleep, inert, a-tune.

Sunrise, the babe leaps forth,
Moonrise, he meets the maiden,
Tides, he suffers and riots,
Darkness, he recoils and dreams,
Recoils, descends
Toward the image within the image,
To devour the flower of rage,
To eat dust and taste blood,
Tight in the brackish fluid,
Brute, blind, in broken story a slave,
In the cave, the tight cave.

At noon his shadow merges with his fellows,
At noon, he toils and is heavy,
At noon he is slain and made many,
He is dismembered, he is eaten
And of others, he eats.

58877

So he is born of man
In the realm and meaning
Of myriad man. Forgets

MOUNT UNION COLLEGE LIBRARY
ALLIANCE, OHIO

Oblivion, the cave,
Its residue, its after-birth; forgives
The tides their prod, accepts
Penetration of the sane sun; loves
Authority of the task,
Its antagonist fiber; dreams
His deep acquaintance with the stuff of things; adores
The burnished withering moon.

Marvelous now is man.
Wrinkles next his eyes,
Stubs of his ten fingers
Grow the exquisite skin of self.
Odors of love and sweat,
Voices of youthful creatures
Fill cups with winey light
Sweet to the lips; he drinks,
Groans in his excess
Lies prone to procreate.
Within is a great wave cresting,
The glee of the master.
He strides, an exuberant creature,
Happy at pitch, the crescent of his spanning,
Sober, with labor; defeat his skidding shadow.

Adjusted by the moon to wane,
A-down, a-dark,
Rejoicing and desponding,
Elate, afraid, shod with electric spurs,
Petitions not to die.
(For after he is slain his feeling is immortal.)
Mortal, lofty, in him, the human spirit
Repeats, repeats, petitions not to die.

MOUNT UNION COLLEGE LIBRARY
ALLIANCE, OHIO

Hark, and afar he feels return
The tug of tide and sun
The shock of setting moon
In solemn orb and wave, and these reply:
Lie down in nothing's cave,
Obey the grave. Undo thy self. Obey.
Now he is closing,
In mystery withers away.
Half-harking he shrivels, shrinks,
He is cradled, laved.
He is near nothing,
A nothing vast.
Now he is near pure nothing,
He is that nothing he knows never, never,
That nothing that is,
Bliss within bliss
He is no one
He is unspun.
Asleep, inert, a-tune,
A-down, a-dark,
Where pull and fuse
Forces of the tide, moon, sun.
(A gliding tide,
A moon
A swooning sun.)

1945

The Zig Zag Song

EVEN in America
One can sit under a sycamore tree
And see three ships a-sailing. . . .
So life goes on sedately,
Goes stupidly or greatly,
Goes crookedly or straightly,
And the sycamore grows without fail.

And in Iowa I saw
A partridge in a pear tree.
A ballad is often what it used to be,
Bitterly or greatly,
Crookedly or straightly
The image will dance sedately,
Although desire fail. . . .

(Darling, those who made the wilful songs of old
Were often poor and cold.)

1945

Date Due

MAY 1 4 '49			